DANIEL LIBESKIND

Inspiration and Process in Architecture

Edited by
Francesca Serrazanetti, Matteo Schubert

Published by Moleskine SpA

Series and Book Editors
Francesca Serrazanetti, Matteo Schubert

Publishing Director
Roberto Di Puma

Publishing Coordinator
Igor Salmi

Graphic design
A+G AchilliGhizzardiAssociati

ISBN 978-88-6732-479-8

Text "From a point to a line: how drawing informs
the architectural practice of Daniel Libeskind"
by Danielle Rago
Other texts by Francesca Serrazanetti

First edition October 2015
Printed in Italy by Galli Thierry

We would like to thank
Studio Libeskind
Amanda de Beaufort, director of communications
Lana Barkin, communications coordinator

Inspiration and Process in Architecture is a series of monographs on key figures in modern
and contemporary architecture. It offers a reading of the practice of design which emphasises
the value of freehand drawing as part of the creative process. Each volume provides a different
perspective, revealing secrets and insights and showing the various observation techniques
languages, characters, forms and means of communication.

Contents

MILFORD · CONN 19 - 36 - 54
FOLD - UN - FOLD

18.36.56
Connecticut, USA, 2010
sketch

Writings

Architectural explorations
and design process in drawings

Is architectural drawing no more than a working tool, a design process that leads to a finished product, or is it in itself an architectural quest, independent of the shape it takes in physical terms? For Daniel Libeskind it is both, and it is difficult to determine which of these two aspects has had more of an impact on his professional career. It is clear that Libeskind approached architecture through the practice of drawing, as exemplified by the series of works which he himself refuses to call "theoretical" since they are in themselves architecture, as he has pointed out several times in his writings and reaffirms in the interview featured in the following pages. In the course of his career, architecture visualized through a quasi-philosophical paradigm has been continuously alternated with concrete design. While the former involves non-figurative images that plumb the primal depths of the discipline, the latter consists of sketches and insights tirelessly taken down on paper and exhibiting their own unmistakeable expressive language, capable of transcending mere representation and conveying the deeper meaning of the project.

It was in 1979, in the text entitled *End Space* accompanying the *Micromegas* drawings, that Libeskind stated, "An architectural drawing is as much a prospective unfolding of future possibilities as it is a recovery of a particular history to whose intentions it testifies and whose limits it always challenges. In any case a drawing is more than the shadow of an object, more than a pile of lines, more than a resignation to the inertia of convention."[1] This signals the book's point of departure: that first series in which we recognize the "signature" of the Polish-American architect and which heralds the definitive arrival of Libeskind the musician in the world of architecture. In selecting those drawings most capable of illustrating the

[1] Daniel Libeskind, *End Space: An exhibition at the Architectural Association*, The Architectural Association, London, 1980, p. 22.

web of inspirations and processes at play in his work, we decided to systematically alternate those which constitute works in their own right as "architectural explorations" – *Micromegas* (1979), *Chamber Works* (1983), and *Sonnets in Babylon* (2011) – and those tied to the designing process of a few commissioned works of "real" architecture. The latter are merged into three categories that serve to systematize Libeskind's different approaches to the dimensions of the project: the "grafts" of new interventions onto historical buildings, often with museum-oriented purposes linked to the deeper history of the city and which require a scrupulous treatment of the project on a more reduced scale, from the Jewish Museum Berlin to the expansion of the Victoria and Albert Museum in London, all the way to the Dresden Military History Museum; the urban projects that display a similar sensitivity regarding the "stitching" of fragments into the heart of the city, from the master plan for the Potsdamer Platz in Berlin to that of the World Trade Center in New York; and finally, the tower-high projections that signal a more recent and controversial phase of Libeskind's work, from the Green New York Tower to the Zlota in Warsaw.

What at first blush might appear as a convoluted career attempting to unite contradictory and diverging paths in fact adheres to a fervently experimental logic which, running along parallel lines of abstraction and practice, allows one to investigate human existence and experience through architecture in the knowledge that one's conception of reality can in no way be reconciled to a single discourse.

Looking at the drawings in this book which range from 1979 to 2014, one immediately notices how the mark of Libeskind is uniquely identifiable in both categories, and therefore confirms the assertion of the architect: "theoretical" research underpins the practice of design; it is the mental inquiry that nourishes the construction of buildings. Throughout the 1980s, Libeskind's references included Peter Eisenman, John Hejduk and Aldo Rossi. These figures' influence directed him to ensure that theory would not be divorced from practice but could create its own vocabulary of reference. Indeed, it is a vocabulary that is more concrete than it may at first appear, anticipating a subsequent career as a designer who would immediately assume intellectual stature and an unfailing recognizability. In studies such as *Micromegas* and *Chamber Works*, that which may seem to be a series of chaotic lines or exercises in deconstruction is actually an attempt to seek out new systems, new coherent orders capable of rendering on paper the complexity of a space surgically penetrated by the gaze of its author. "Drawing is a graphic technique that serves to reduce the complexity of real space and is not a representation or reproduction thereof."[2]

It is with the Jewish Museum Berlin, where he is offered the chance to test the third dimension, that Libeskind is able put his theories to the test. From that moment on there follow a series of projects in which a personal "generative blueprint" takes shape, composed of axes and lines that intersect, where the entanglements and ligatures generate suspensions charged with meaning. These spaces invariably defy immediate comprehension.

Inspiration and process are therefore two vital aspects born of both theoretical and practical speculations, and from which dialogue with the arts draws its value as a matrix. The ability to involve stimuli from a variety of disciplines and world cultures (not only the arts) in the architectural process is one of Libeskind's most distinctive traits: for him architecture is a field inseparable from philosophy, music, art, literature, astronomy, graphology, geology, history... Thus, in the Jewish Museum we find a reference to the music of Arnold Schoenberg; the Grand Canal Theatre in Dublin draws inspiration from James Joyce's *Finnegans Wake*; the trajectory of the sun's motion guides the project of Ground Zero and the Tower of

[2] Attilio Terragni, *Daniel Libeskind, oltre i muri*, Testo & Immagine, Torino, 2001, p. 20.

Warsaw, while xenomorphous crystals shape the expressive language of the Royal Ontario Museum in Toronto and the CityCenter of Las Vegas, and so forth.

The work of Daniel Libeskind, therefore, confirms that architectural drawing does not simply represent something that is external to itself – as in, buildings that have been or are to be constructed – but is in itself a creative work. If the materials published in the three "design-oriented" chapters of this book constitute clues to be interpreted by the team intent on defining the project, the others are consummate works of architecture (or is it art?). The autographic or allographic[3] dimension of architectural drawing can be seen to overlap and coincide once again at this juncture. It's no coincidence that the drawings classified as "explorations" in the summary of the architect's published works on his website are defined as "completed".

[3] Cf. the distinction proposed by Nelson Goodman in his *Languages of Arts: An Approach to a Theory of Symbols*, Hackett Publishing Company, Indianapolis, 1976.

From a point to a line: how drawing informs the architecture practice of Daniel Libeskind

Danielle Rago

Approaching the architecture of Daniel Libeskind through his drawings is the only way to fully appreciate and understand his practice. His prolific library (adjacent to his architectural office) houses an encyclopedic collection of ancient architectural treatises, Baroque doctrines of Bernini, Borromini and Guarini, the etchings of Piranesi, doctrines by Perrault and Durand, among many other texts that continue to inspire and inform Libeskind's architectural practice. Delving through layers of history, theory and culture, Libeskind's architecture has certainly developed from a cross-section of history and the line of his pen.

Discovering architecture through his mastery of drawing and music [Libeskind was a young virtuoso of the accordion at an early age], Libeskind tells me, "Architecture combined all my true interests. I only changed my instruments."
Having received a professional degree in architecture from the Cooper Union for the Advancement of Science and Art, studying under architectural masters such as John Hejduk, Peter Eisenman, Richard Meier, and Bauhaus artist Hannes Beckman, among many other visionaries; Libeskind didn't take the traditional route of an architectural ingénue by apprenticing at various architectural firms after graduation [although he briefly worked at Richard Meier's office and Peter Eisenman's New York Institute for Architecture and Urban Studies]. He instead decided to forge a different path, one that took him through academic or theoretical work.

Upon graduating, the young architect decided to move to England to pursue other studies. At the University of Essex in the School of Comparative Studies, Libeskind studied the History and Theory of Architecture. This program opened his mind to the study of other disciplines beyond that of architecture, subjects such as astronomy, archeology, poetry, and philosophy. It was there, in England, that Libeskind first began develop his sensibility for architecture and his ability to see architecture as he sees it now, as a humanistic discipline. Approaching the discipline from this new point-of-view at this time [in the 1970s] was a radical thought considering the discipline's long-standing interest in modernist ideals and principles. Libeskind was later an instrumental figure in shifting architectural education away from traditional ideas about building.

Using drawing to communicate his ideas and thoughts into practice, drawing was the architect's chosen métier. To Libeskind, nothing will ever replace the sense of creation with the hand, the eye and mind. His process remains very much the same today, first drawing by hand and then making very modest models sometimes out of paper that are very primitive looking.

This understanding and application of drawing can be traced back to the first set of published work by the architect in 1979, his infamous *Micromegas* drawings, named after a satirical short story by Voltaire and consisting of eleven pencil drawings which served as a study for a series of twelve prints that explored the relationship between drawing and the process of construction. In *Micromegas*, Libeskind created dynamic three-dimensional spatial compositions consisting of fragments that have been reassembled and ordered to construct a synthetic whole.[4] "Libeskind's drawing inhaled in a single breath the history of modern drawing, from Piranesi through Kandinsky to Held, and breathed out a typhoon of originality."[5] This drawing suite, exhibited as part of the 1988 landmark exhibition *Deconstructivist Architecture* at the Museum of Modern Art in New York, organized by Philip Johnson and Mark Wigley, established Libeskind as a visionary archi-

[4] Jennifer A.E. Shields, *Collage and Architecture*, Routledge, New York, 2014, p. 80.
[5] Jeffrey Kipnis, *Preface* to Daniel Libeskind, *The Space of Encounter*, Universe Publishing, New York, 2000, p. 10.

tect who was using drawing as a way to redefine the limits and purpose of architectural representation and in doing so, explore "new ideas of space and its human purposes than are afforded by the ordinary design process based on history and accepted building typologies."[6]

His second set of palimpsest drawings from 1983 titled *Chamber Works, Architectural Mediations on Themes from Heraclitus*, further abstracted and more highly synthesized, using line only to imply depth and hierarchy without defining discreet formal fragments.[7] This set of twenty-eight drawings was an architectonic and graphic interplay between music and architecture. According to Libeskind, "I explored through my work [...] a more exposed investigation of the ideas of architecture and music as they intersect in the chamber of the mind."[8] *Chamber Works* has been subject to much critique and investigation from the time they were published to present-day mostly on account of Libeskind's radical approach to architectural drawing and more importantly, his advanced and critical thinking of the subject. Robin Evans noted in an essay from the *AA Files* in May 1984 that the drawings "do not move toward unity, nor are they subject to fragmentation. It took me a while to realize that there was nothing to be broken [...] no subject matter [...] Lines that do not make bodies cannot be broken."[9] Almost twenty years later in 2000, architecture critic Jeff Kipnis remarked that the drawings were performing "an eccentric history of the architect's sine qua non, the straight line" and more specifically as "an embryogeny, the development of that genetic diagram into the material specificity of an individual, the line in and as Daniel."[10]

This drawing suite, consisting of *Micromegas* and *Chamber Works*, developed the language and technique of line that would ultimately drive the architect's future proposals and built work; from his proposal for the City Edge Competition in Berlin (1987) which conceptually addresses line to his winning competition entry in 1988 for the Jewish Museum Berlin, that catapulted the architect's

[6] Lebbeus Woods, *Libeskind's Machines*, November 24, 2009.
[7] Jennifer A.E. Shields, *ibidem*.
[8] Daniel Libeskind, *op. cit.*, p. 52.
[9] Robin Evans, *In Front of Lines That Leave Nothing Behind*, in "AA Files" 6, 1984.
[10] Jeffrey Kipnis, *op. cit.*, p. 12.

career and officially began his eponymous architectural practice, Studio Libeskind. Prior to the Jewish Museum Berlin commission, Libeskind had never built a building before but even when, explains Libeskind, "I was doing what seemed to others to be abstract drawings, I never thought of them as theoretical but as somehow part of an investigation of architecture."[11]

This investigation of architecture – it's history, philosophy, broader socio-political meaning, has been at the crux of the architect's career over the past thirty years. In doing so, he utilizes drawing as a critical tool to carry out this systematic and formal inquiry of discovery and examination of subject and place. At the Jewish Museum Berlin, for example, the architect "transformed the entire structure into a discourse about German-Jewish history."[12] Affectionately called, "Between the Lines" by Libeskind, the Jewish Museum Berlin is about two different lines of thinking, organization, and relationship. One line is a straight line, but broken into many fragments; the other is a torturous line, but continuing indefinitely.[13] Context here is critical: the Museum's heavily contested site: in Berlin, Germany, its subject: the Holocaust, and lastly, the complex web of relationships between the Germans and Jewish people. Starting here, at the humanistic level, Libeskind creates a dialogue through his design that exposes context through deliberate techniques of erasure, void, shifts, tilts, and fissure.

Here, Libeskind employs line again, but instead of using pen he etches a matrix, which bears reference to the Star of David, into the zinc façade of the building and plots the addresses of prominent Jewish and German citizens on a map of prewar Berlin, stressing the interconnections between these two seemingly different groups of people. Upon entering the Museum, visitors will come to find the interior space is just as charged if not more than its exterior counterpart. Entering through the original Baroque building of the Berlin Museum, guests descend by stair-

[11] Daniel Libeskind, Paul Goldberger, *Counterpoint: Daniel Libeskind in conversation with Paul Goldberger*, The Monacelli Press, New York, 2008, p. 8.
[12] *Ibidem*, p. 22.
[13] Daniel Libeskind, *op. cit.*, p. 23.

way through the dramatic Entry Void into the new museum. A narrative creates the pathway of the visitor's experience through the Museum space. Three underground "roads" symbolize three paths in the history of German Jews. The first leads to the Holocaust Tower, which is a dead end that is lit by a single narrow slit high above the ground; the second to the Garden of Exile and Emigration, a memorial designed for those forced to leave Berlin; and the third to the Stair of Continuity which connects the museum to the central exhibition space and signifies a continuous history. A zigzag plan cuts a void through the new building and creates an interstitial space that can be read as absence. In order to navigate from one side of the museum to the other, visitors must physically encounter this seemingly violent slash through the building by crossing one of the sixty bridges that open up onto this void. This regulating line, "its choice and the modalities of expression given to it are an integral part of architectural creation."[14] Constantly negotiating between line – in elevation, plan and section, visitors are confronted with contradictions between old and new [building], past and present [history], fissure and continuity [in both], which is very much part of the narrative of the history of Berlin, the meaning of the Holocaust, and the acknowledgement and incorporation of this erasure and void of Jewish life in Berlin.[15]

"Architectural space", as the architect remarked in a 2008 interview with Paul Goldberger, "has to be part of the story it's trying to communicate. It's not just a container to be filled; it's part of the symbolism of the building. And the symbol transports you beyond the material reality and, in architecture, toward that which language itself cannot fully articulate."[16] The limitation of architectural language in terms of the traditional use of the terms "form" "function" and "program" are limiting here. By instead engaging in another realm – the social and political, the building takes on a new dimension with inherent social meaning for a people, a culture, and a place.

[14] Le Corbusier, *Towards a New Architecture*, [Paris, 1923] Dover Publications, New York, 1986, p. 3.
[15] Daniel Libeskind, *op. cit.*, p. 23.
[16] Daniel Libeskind, Paul Goldberger, *op. cit.*, p. 14.

Libeskind has gone on to design countless projects at various scales from large-scale civic projects in the United States and Europe, sacred sites in the Middle East, large-scale urban planning projects in Asia, to small objects, furnishings and fixtures for brands like Alessi, Artemide, Jacuzzi, Poliform, among others. While the size of the project may differ what remains constant is the architect's steadfast approach to design and an overarching humanistic principle to guide everything that he touches from initial sketch to final product. For Libeskind, as he told me, "everything is really architecture... just at different scales."

Interview with Daniel Libeskind

❝ *In this book, the sketches relating to the design of a building alternate with drawings that are used for theoretical research, as tools to investigate architecture – for instance* Micromegas, Chamber Works, Sonnets in Babylon. *Would you define this second typology as "theoretical drawings"? What do they represent for you, and how are the two types linked to each other?*

I would not consider them theoretical, even thought they don't seem to have an immediately applicable figurative meaning for architecture. They are conceived as *structural explorations* of both spatial and functional aspects of the experience of buildings or cities. I've drawn them at different times of my life, but I never thought of them as theoretical but as drawings to be used, and I continue to use them. They are not something I do to display at architecture exhibitions; I use this type of drawing to develop three-dimensional tectonic constructions. They are part of that research and the love that I have for drawings of different kinds.

By the way, it's not so different from the Renaissance tradition: when you look at the drawings of the Renaissance masters or later works, you find all sorts of styles. There might be a drawing of a human figure, there might be a calculation, a perspective of an unexpected imaginary construction, or a machine. They are all drawings in the spirit of the humanistic tradition – they are not immediately implemented in a sort of machinery of practice, they're definitely the other side of practice; they are the source, in many ways, of buildings. Take for example the *Chamber* drawings, which are currently in the exhibition on art and music at the Museum of Modern Art in New York. The starting point of these was the relationship between music and the structure of architecture; *Micromegas* and *Sonnets in Babylon* were developed in a different way, but they all are interrelated with architectural ideas.

66 *Speaking of music, before beginning your career as an architect, you studied and practised music at a professional level. How do these two fields influence each other? And what relationship do you see between the sketch in architecture and the score in music?*

I don't even consider them separate fields: they are both architectural. Both music and architecture rely on a coded system of communication: a music notation or a plan drawing or a master-plan drawing. At the same time they both involve such incredible precision as to require specific skills of interpretation, whether a performance or a construction. The mathematical and geometric precision of both music and architecture in their communicative systems merge to evoke an emotional response, not a mechanical response, even though they are most often mechanically drawn. So I find the way in which music and architecture are produced almost identical.

Think of my Ground Zero master plan: it's a series of drawings which are very precise, in every sense, just as a musical score is. I'm not the person who's playing a violin or a cello or a drum or a trumpet: as a conductor I'm not even visible to the public; but the large teams of architects and engineers are a kind of orchestra that has to interpret these drawings, within a certain range of freedom, otherwise it would be a mechanical process – there would be no realness to it. There is a certain range of interpretation for these very precise marks. Both in system and in spirit, music and architecture are similar: music produces a structure in sound and time, and architecture produces a structure in space and time.

I see them really as the same kind of "vibration": when I press a pencil to a piece of paper, it's like pressing a finger to a keyboard.

66 *Is there any other discipline – apart from music – that has influenced your work?*

Definitely – I think the whole field of human expression: the humanities, poetry, dance, geometry, astronomy, mechanics, the sciences and the arts. Because that's architecture to me: it's a cultural discipline; despite the fact that it's scientific, it's cultural, fundamentally.

66 *Going back to the years of your education, which people most influenced your work? Who would you consider to be your "masters" or your basic reference points?*

I was lucky at school. I studied in New York and I had teachers like Peter Eisenman, Richard Mayer, John Hejduk, a great poet and architect who was a strong supporter of my work. But of course I had other guides, too, like James Stirling, the Japanese architects, the work of Le Corbusier, Frank Lloyd Wright, Alvar Aalto... There's an entire legacy and my masters also go back in time. In my library I have treaties by Borromini, Guarini, Alberti and other ancient writings. Today the entire tradition of architecture is available to inspire one, and I often pore over the treaties of John Soane on the question of light and walls.

66 *So, architectural drawing is an important tool of research in architecture, employed at different phases of the design process or during personal research. In this sense it is different from drawing as it is used in other disciplines such as art. What is the main role of this tool for you?*

To me, drawing is the spark of architecture; it's a spark that fans into a flame that illuminates what you are doing. I always start with a drawing, and drawing to me is both practical and mystical. It's a sort of connection between the poetry of the hand and the eye of the mind, from which something is created. It's really the source of my belief: that's where architecture comes from. A drawing calls on such depth of inspiration and practice: starting a drawing has always been something I've loved, even making drawings, constructing drawings, of a building that might never be built.

" A drawing can also represent in a few lines the very essence of a project, reducing it to its core. Would you tell us about how you communicate your ideas by transcribing concepts into sketches, usually generating kinds of "icons" of your projects?

It all starts with the drawing, before words come into play. You have to connect yourself to the vision through drawing, and out of the lines comes something that you can't name till later, when you make more drawings and a small physical model. Then you work with incredible creative teams to translate it into more technical information through the computer, 3D visualization, virtual reality and so on.

But it's always something very primal that informs the first sketch, whether it's made on a piece of paper, on a boarding pass, or on an iPad, which I also use.

" How do you develop the observation of the context at the beginning of the project? What affects the subsequent design research most?

Probably it's how you draw the site and what you draw. You don't draw a normal landscape that shows all the grass and the sky; you pick out only what it's really about. You can draw a face without any eyes and it can be more expressive than a face with eyes and eyebrows.

This is one of the fundamentals of drawing: what your eye and mind capture and transmit onto the page might not look anything like the reality. A drawing is an individual mindscape. It's as if a cross-section appears in your brain of what's there for you in what you're looking at.

" Some of the projects that appear in this book are like "diamonds" grafted onto existing buildings – the Jewish Museum, the Military History Museum, the Royal Ontario Museum – while on the urban scale you design master plans that are like incisions in the soul of the city. The relationship between the past and the new, between the drawing and the realized building, happens through the contrast of new shadows and new materials. Can you tell us something about this kind of adaptive process?

It's not a matter of trying to be nostalgic or sentimental, an attempt to blend history into a picture of the past that is soothing, but of trying to show the elements of history. Often they are contradictory elements that shift as time passes, and the opposition in the contrasts produces a completely different configuration of how we relate to time. I've never tried to obliterate the era in which a building was built; of course certain special constructions and figures emerge out of the conversation between traditional buildings and the contemporary buildings of today.

❝ *How has the role of drawing been transformed during the course of your career, including in relation to the first theoretical investigations, and in view of the huge potential represented by graphic modelling and three-dimensional elaboration on computer?*

I think the methods used today are all tools, whether you have a pencil in your hand, or whether you use your finger on the screen of an iPad. Any tool, even a violin, demands a technique that you have to master. And it can take years and years. Drawing skill comes through drawing, it comes from studying drawing, and in a strange way it is becoming more fundamental to me as virtual technology becomes more sophisticated. You can represent things now in systems that are almost unbelievable, that can create images of complete buildings in seconds. But because of that, I love the more primordial nature of a drawing, of what the hands can do, whether it's on a screen, on paper, or lines drawn in the sand. A drawing can look "nice", but have a further dimension: it can be just as much a mechanical tool that inspires a real constructed world as a mathematical formulation.

There is something amazing about drawing, and I think it's not coincidence that the verb "to draw" is also used as "to draw water from a well". You *draw* from a well and you also *draw* a card in a cards game. The idea of drawing reaches in many directions and goes a long, long way back. And I think that, in that sense, virtual reality will never supplant how it all started, which is probably by someone drawing, with their finger, a line in the sand dividing one part from another part – maybe at the very origin of geometry. In architecture, that line drawn on a piece of paper, or on a computer, is also ultimately a line in space, a line in the earth, a line of construction, a line of measurement. And it has to be able to work in all those dimensions simultaneously.

Kö-Bogen

Düsseldorf, Germany,
2013
concept drawings

"BOA CONSTRICTORS SWALLOW
THEIR PREY WHOLE, WITHOUT
CHEWING"

"WHY BE SCARED OF A HAT?"

"GROWN-UPS NEVER UNDERSTAND ANYTHING BY THEMSELVES ......"

"A BOA CONSTRICTOR DIGESTING
AN ELEPHANT"

WHY BE SCARED OF BLOCKS.

GROWN-UPS ARE KIDS IN A PARK .....

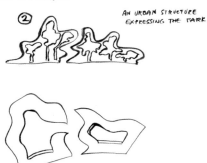

AN URBAN STRUCTURE
EXPRESSING THE PARK

Drawings

Architectural Explorations 1
Micromegas

What may appear as chaotic lines or exercises in deconstruction are often attempts at finding new systems, new
orders. Hence, in *Micromegas*, drawing is a graphic technique which serves to delve into the complexity of real
space, reducing it to abstract lines and shapes and rendering it graphically visible on paper. Bearing the name of
Voltaire's philosophical tale, this inquiry uses drawing to
explore dimensions of space and time: just as in Voltaire's
Micromegas a man eight leagues tall who lives on the enor-
mous planet Sirius with "a name perfectly suited to all great
figures" ends up investigating the nature of the microscopic
inhabitants of Earth, Libeskind's *Micromegas* dissects
space. By shifting the parameters of how reality is read, the
vision explodes and recasts the linguistic instruments to
achieve an unprecedented perspective.

Drawing assumes an experiential role, never isolated but in
sequence, eliciting the perception of the environment that
surrounds the observer like an infinite multiplicity of dark
spaces. Examining space and shapes, the drawing projects
onto paper imaginary places composed of lines that become denser through the sudden quickening of a sketch.
The result is a coherent place in the imagination that has
nothing to do with the practical or with real spaces, similar
to what happens in the impossible constructions of Escher
or the labyrinthine prisons imagined by Piranesi.
Thus, in the drawings that mark the beginning of Libeskind's
career as an architect, a new form of investigation into the
subtler meanings of the discipline takes shape. With a sur-
gical eye, he analytically dissects the microparticles of the
real, exploring the limits of architectural drawing in a sub-
stantial reassessment of the role of this instrument. Every il-
lustration is an explosion of graphic signs and compositional
devices that render indecipherable the perception of depth,
even penetrating the two dimensions of the piece of paper.

Micromegas
drawings, 1979
Cover

Nº 20
Daniel Libeskind

THIS IS :
OF A LIMITED **30**
EDITION OF
NUMBERED AND SIGNED
PORTFOLIOS

micromegas
THE ARCHITECTURE OF END SPACE

D. LIBESKIND

"About the four hundred and fiftieth
year of his age, or latter end of his
childhood, he dissected a great
number of small insects not more
than one hundred feet in diameter,
which are not perceivable by
ordinary microscopes, of which he
composed a very curious
treatise, which involved him in
some trouble."

VOLTAIRE

Hand-Screened by RICHARD GARST at CRANBROOK, 1979

MICROMEGAS

1 THE GARDEN
2 TIME SECTIONS
3 LEAKAGE
4 LITTLE UNIVERSE
5 ARCTIC FLOWERS
6 THE BURROW LAWS
7 DANCE SOUNDS
8 MALDOROR'S EQUATION
9 VERTICAL HORIZON
10 DREAM CALCULUS

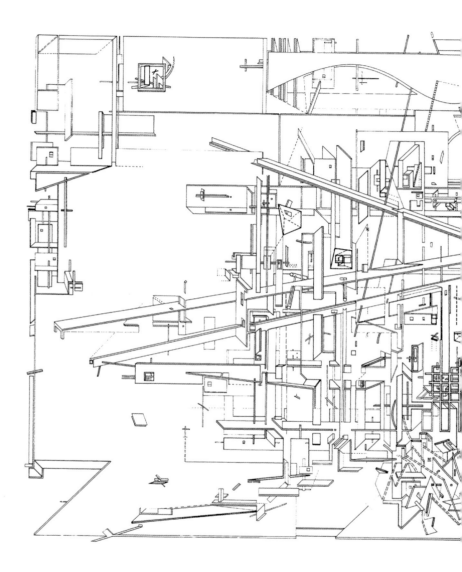

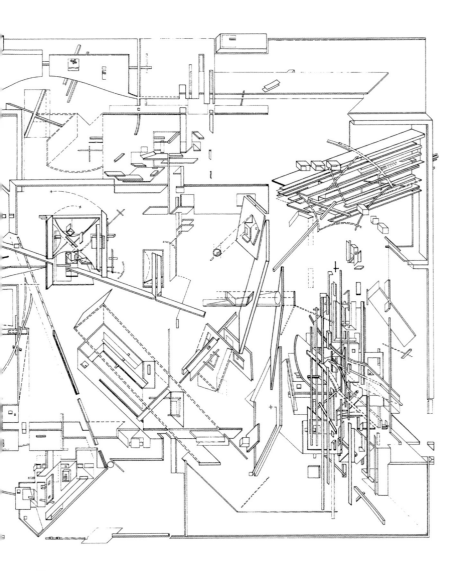

Micromegas
drawings, 1979
The Garden
following pages Time Sections

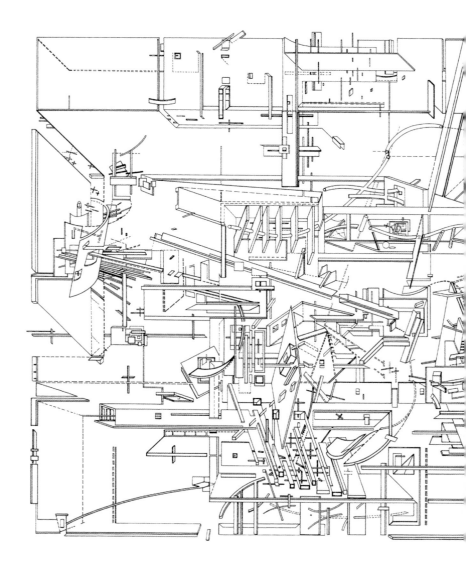

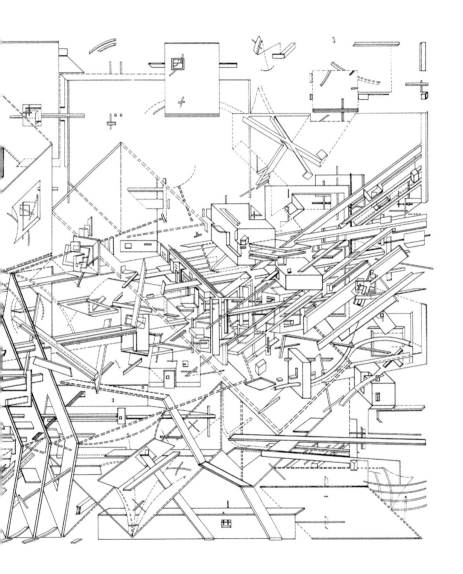

29

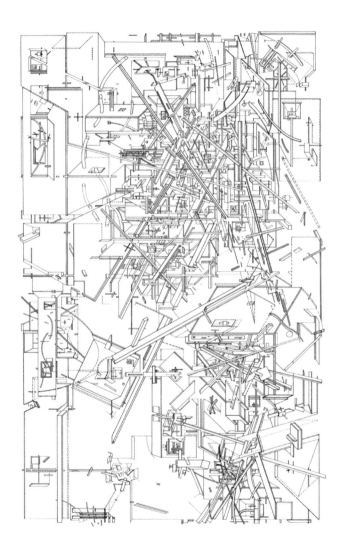

Micromegas
drawings, 1979
left Leakage
right Little Universe

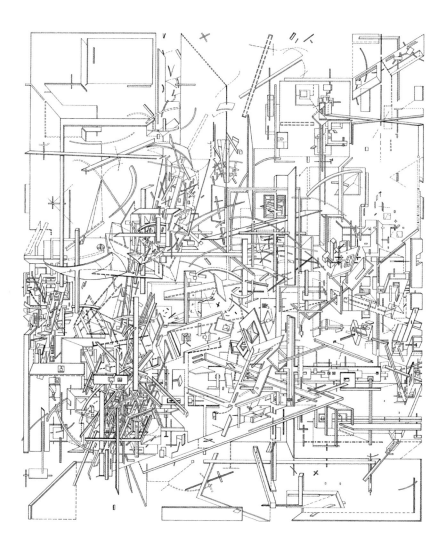

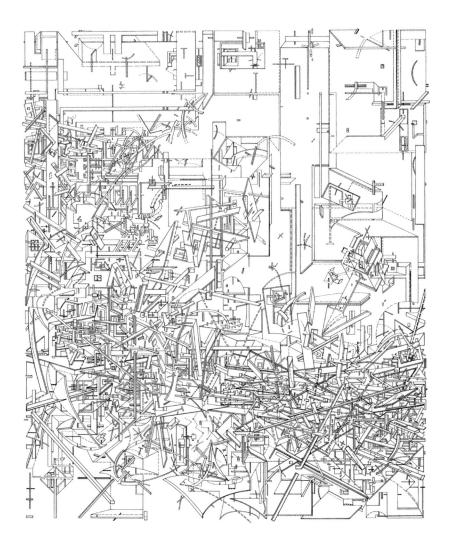

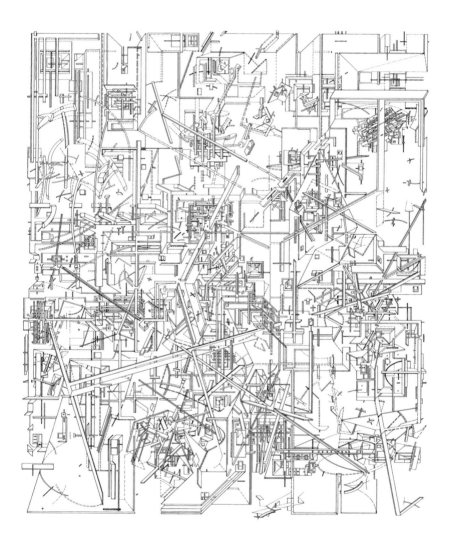

Micromegas
drawings, 1979
left Arctic Flowers
right The Burrow Laws

Micromegas
drawings, 1979
Dance Sounds

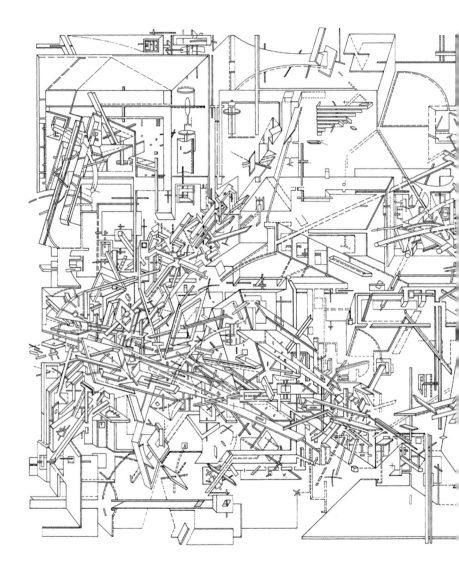

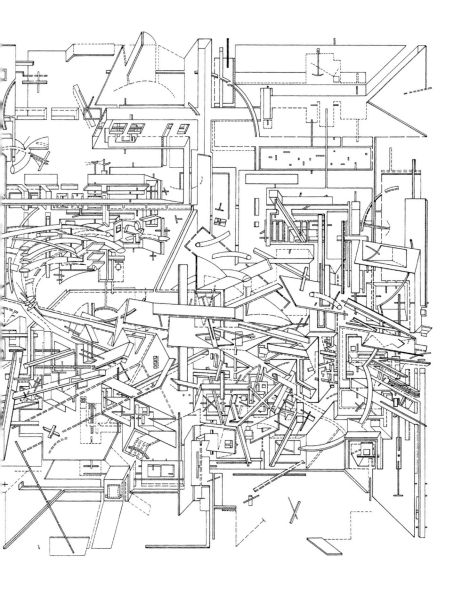

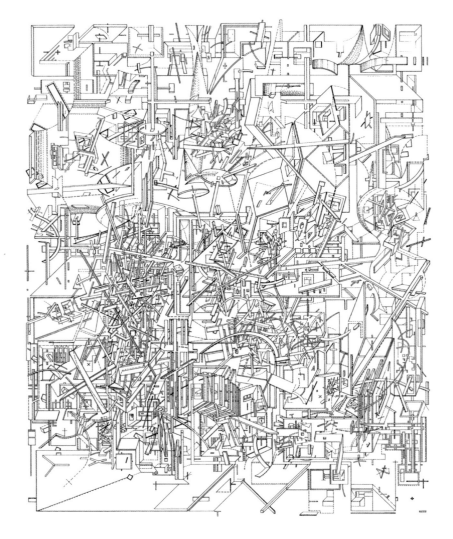

Micromegas
drawings, 1979
left Maldoror's Equation
right Vertical Horizon

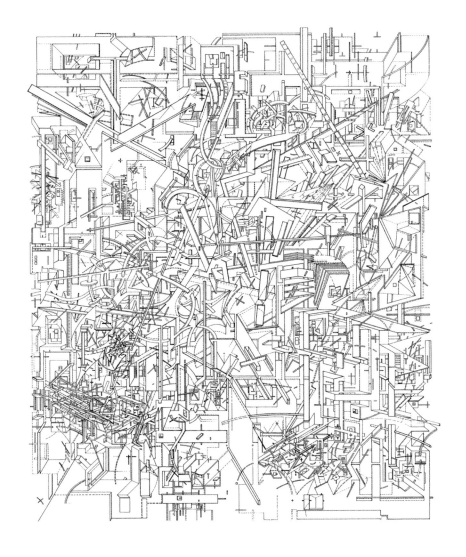

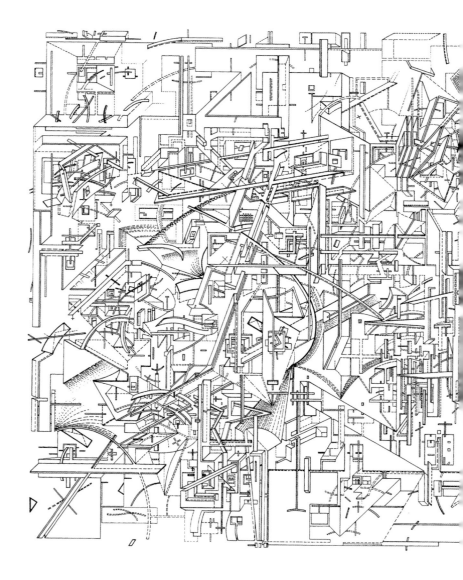

Micromegas
drawings, 1979
Dream Calculus

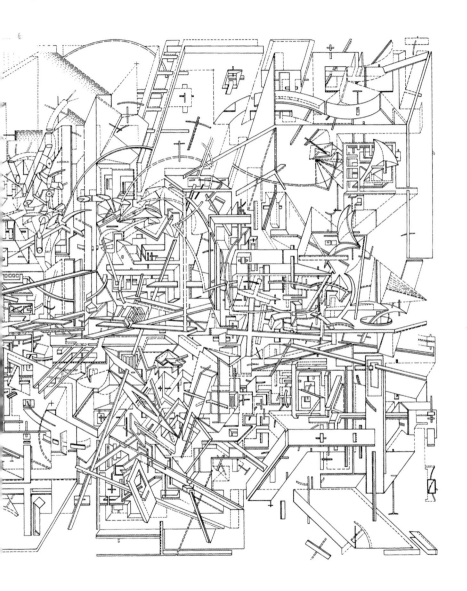

Design Process 1
The lines of complexity

In 1989, Libeskind's quest shifts focus onto the third dimension. The opportunity arises with a commission for the Jewish Museum Berlin. The design of the museum traces lines that seem to emerge from force fields that are invisible but perceptible to a discerning sensibility. In this project, all the experiences and journeys examined previously merge. We witness a transposition from the abstract to the architectural plane by way of inspirations and processes that attest to how Libeskind's architecture is continually nourished by increasingly intellectual disciplines and practices. The matrices become stratified and take shape: the music of Austrian composer Schoenberg and his unfinished opera *Moses and Aaron*, the names of the Berlin Jews deported during the Holocaust, Walter Benjamin's *One-Way Street*, the explosion of a Star of David in a zigzagging line. The intersection of the zigzagging line with a straight one creates a void, just as every point of contact inside a construction forms a node, an interruption that recalls the darkness of a dramatic historical period like the Holocaust.

Those "invisible" lines that serve as the starting point for Libeskind's projects, interweaving with each other at different angles, generate shapes whose external boundaries are not immediately comprehensible. From one project to another the architect grows ever bolder, and the customary designs become increasingly intricate. The generative axes are no longer straight, but bend and unbend to such an extent that in the expansion of the Victoria and Albert Museum they become a spiral. This tendency towards the infinite "Escheresque" matrices, discernible in Libeskind's work, signals a turning point in his method that will be apparent in all subsequent projects: like the intricate and multifaceted prisms set in this historical city with an unmistakeable formal language made of broken lines, shafts of light and walls that defy all criteria of orthogonality.

Between the lines
Jewish Museum
Berlin, Germany, 1999
sketch of the interior, view from the new
building to the existing one

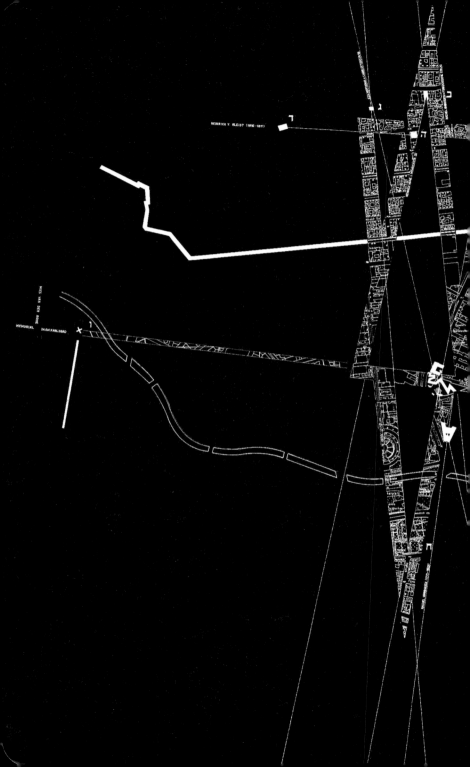

HEINRICH V. KLEIST (1810-1811)

MIES VAN DER ROHE
MEMORIAL
34 AM RAILROAD

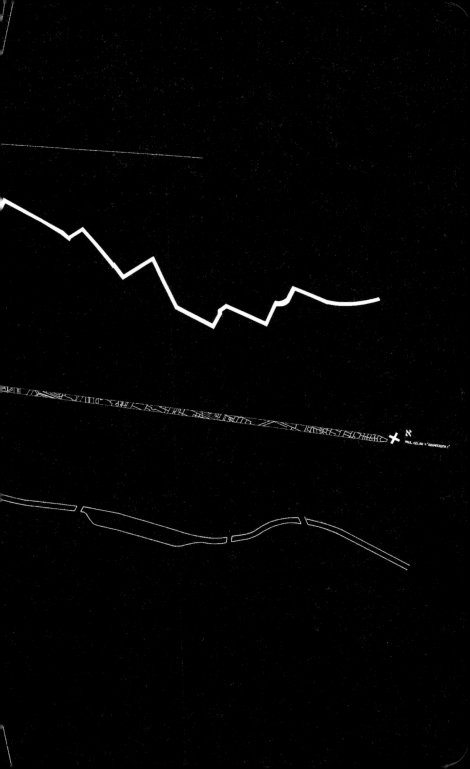

PAUL CELAN = "ORANIENSTR. L"

Between the lines
Jewish Museum
Berlin, Germany, 1999
previous pages Star Matrix
left plan studies
right underground model

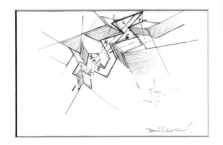

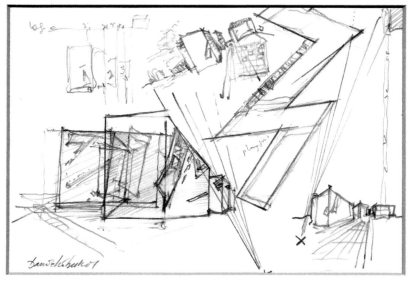

Between the lines
Jewish Museum
Berlin, Germany, 1999
façade sketch

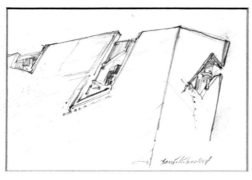

Between the lines
Jewish Museum
Berlin, Germany, 1999
left sketches of the interior
right exterior views

Between the lines
Jewish Museum
Berlin, Germany, 1999
left urban site model
right sketch

51

Between the lines
Jewish Museum
Berlin, Germany, 1999
Composition studies

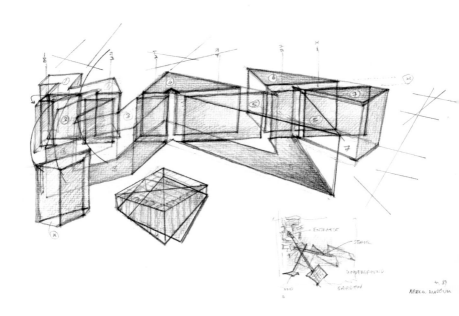

Berlin Museum 89

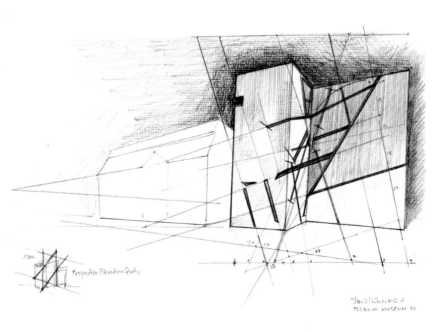

Projection Elevation Study

Daniel Libeskind
Berlin Museum 90

**Between the lines
Jewish Museum**
Berlin, Germany,
1999
Names model -
model of the fullest
development of the
project; the base is
a surface of collaged
names taken from the
pages of the 'geden-
kbuch', a disturbing
compendium of the
names, dates and
places of birth, places
of incarceration, dates
of extermination
and causes of death
of those Germans
who also happened
to be Jews.

Extension to the Victoria and Albert Museum
London, UK, 1996
watercolors

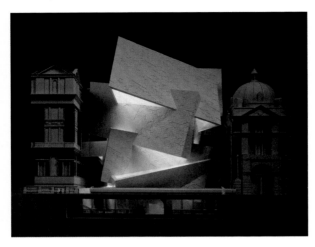

**Extension to the
Victoria and Albert
Museum**
London, UK, 1996
above left model
below left watercolor
right funding sketch

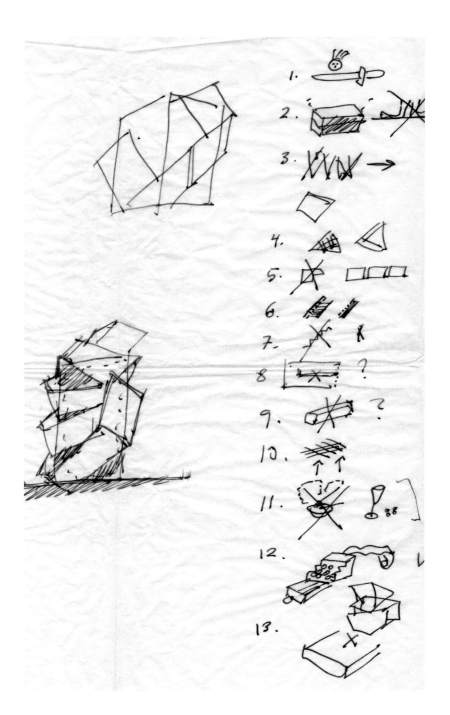

1.

2.

3. →

4.

5.

6.

7.

8. ?

9. ?

10.

11.

12.

13.

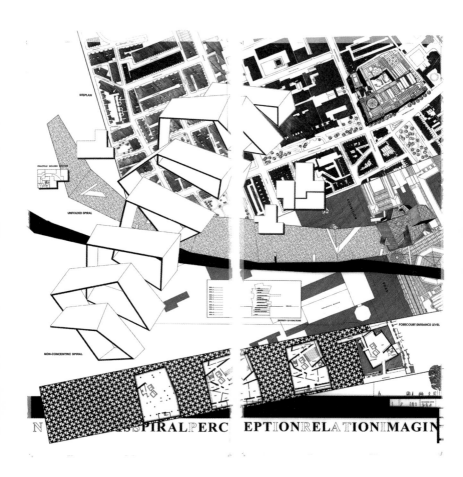

SITEPLAN

FRACTILE GOLDEN

UNFOLDED SPIRAL

NON-CONCENTRIC SPIRAL

DIVERSITY OF FUNCTIONS

FORECOURT ENTRANCE LEVEL

N   SSPIRALPERC EPTIONRELATIONIMAGIN

Extension to the Victoria and Albert Museum
London, UK, 1996
planning presentation panels

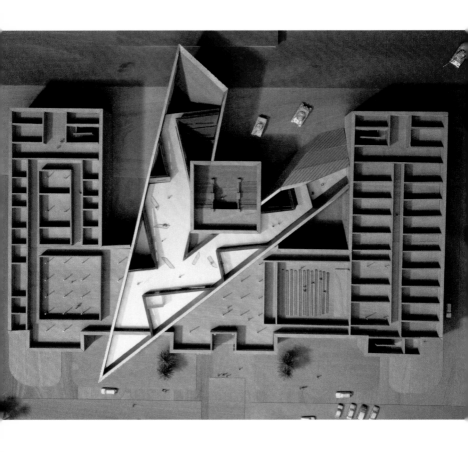

Military History Museum
Dresden, Germany, 2011
left model
right sketches

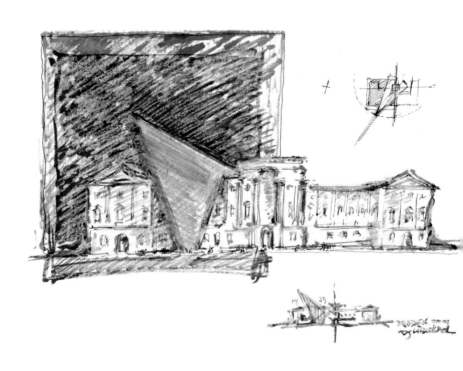

Military History Museum
Dresden, Germany, 2011
elevation studies

**Royal Ontario
Museum**
Toronto, Canada, 2007
left sketch
right model

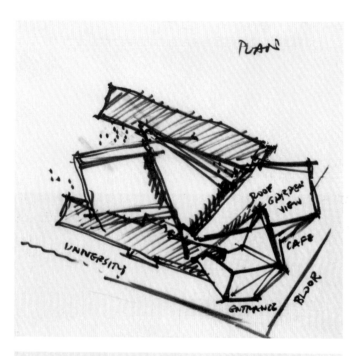

PLAN

ROOF GARDEN VIEW

CAFE

UNIVERSITY

ENTRANCE

BLOOR

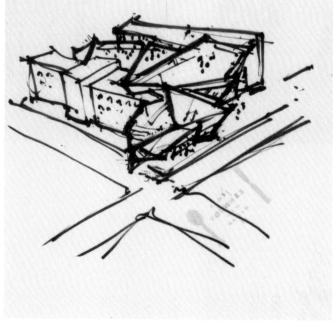

**Royal Ontario
Museum**
Toronto, Canada, 2007
left study sketches
above right study
model
below right sketch

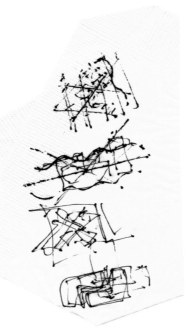

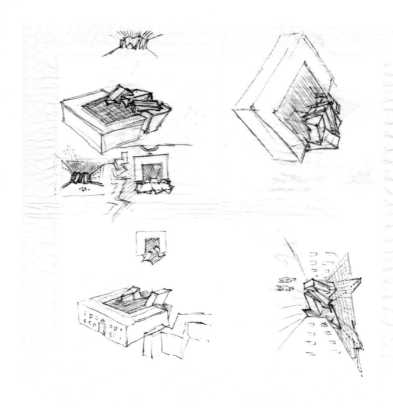

Royal Ontario Museum
Toronto, Canada, 2007
study sketches

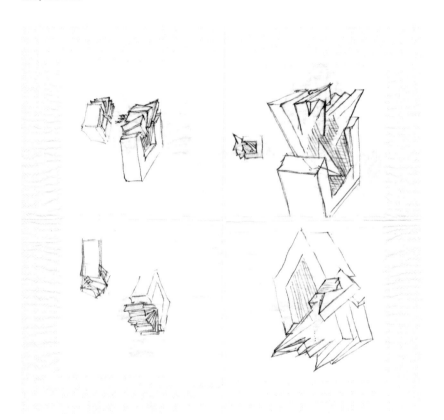

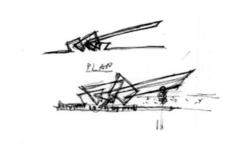

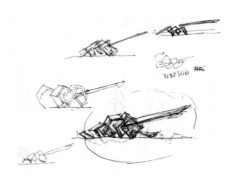

**Extension to the
Denver Art Museum,
Frederic C. Hamilton
Building**
Denver, CO, 2004
left sketches sent
by fax
right composition
studies

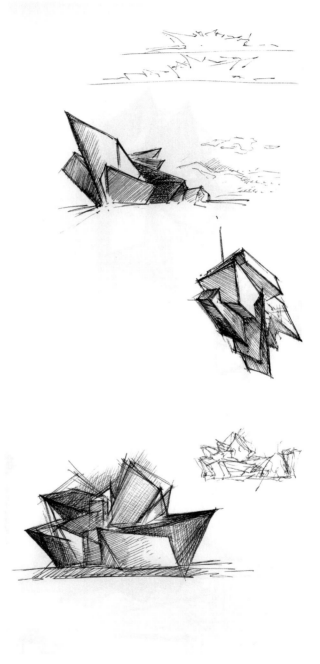

**Extension to the Denver Art Museum,
Frederic C. Hamilton Building**
Denver, CO, 2004
study sketches

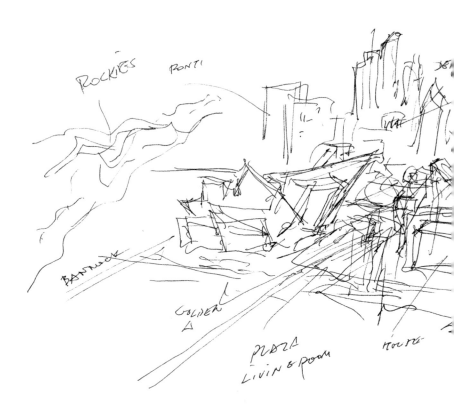

ROCKIES

PONTI

BANDOCK

GOLDEN
△

PLAZA
LIVING ROOM

HOUSE

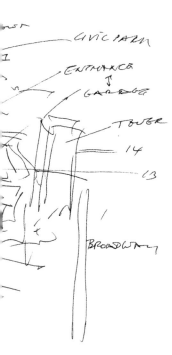

**Extension to the Denver Art Museum,
Frederic C. Hamilton Building**
Denver, CO, 2004
urban views

Architectural Explorations 2
Chamber Works

"The thunderbolt pilots all things," declares a fragment written by Heraclitus. This serves as the point of departure for *Chamber Works: Architectural Meditations on the Themes from Heraclitus*, a series of twenty-eight drawings whose title evokes the creative intimacy of "chamber music" and ways in which music and architecture converge in the mind. Once again, visual representation and any "resemblance" is eschewed. Involving a telescope directed at different registers of the mark, this approach produces a new type of architectural entity. In this case the limits of the plane and the two dimensions are explored in even more radical fashion than in *Micromegas*. Here there is no trace of representation in any spatial sense, but the lines follow autonomous paths independent of any geometric rule. Presented at the Architectural Association at a 1983 exhibition, these drawings were introduced by texts written by Libeskind's masters: Aldo Rossi, Peter Eisenman, John Hejduk and Kurt Forster. They defined them as hieroglyphics (Rossi), illustrations of a thought process and images of the soul (Hejduk), a form of writing (Eisenman), spatial or amorphous musical scores (Forster). The proportion of height to length of the drawings goes from 2:1 to 200:1, until it nearly becomes a single line. Divided into two series of 14 drawings, they can be read either in sequence from 1 to 14, or coupled in such a way that their sum is always 15 (1 with 14, 2 with 13, and so on), evoking Pythagoras, alluded to by Libeskind himself through a quote by Heraclitus as "the prince of impostors". The complexity of *Chamber Works* is defined by Aldo Rossi as "a work in which intellectual, mathematical and speculative elements are interwoven and combined in a kind of formal chaos".

following pages
Chamber Works
Vertical series
Drawings, 1983

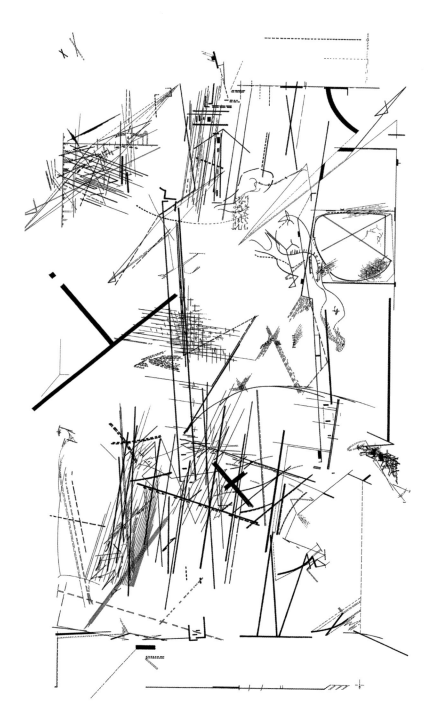

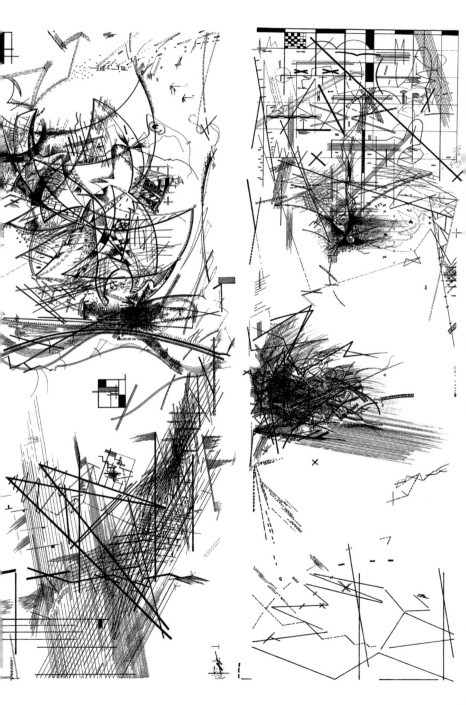

Design Process 2
Urban studies

Libeskind's projects follow a series of "emotional" and cultural references which justify the audacious lines typical of his formal language. This is most clearly expressed in the master plans and the urban-scale studies. The ideas, metaphors and conceptual references translate into a stratification of signs that give shape to new urban structures.

If the concept of a "site-as-puzzle" traces the symbolic fragments of the memory of Potsdamer Platz, recorded from nine vantage points with accelerated temporal perspectives that nullify every prospective conception, the master plan for Ground Zero keeps alive the memory of the disaster in its references to the symbols of Manhattan at the moment tragedy struck, to the Declaration of Independence, and to the poetry of Walt Whitman. While the first urban drawings recall the spatial research in which the lines lose themselves in the complexity of a quasi-abstract inquiry, in later plans the project hides behind schemes which attempt to probe the "soul" of the places.

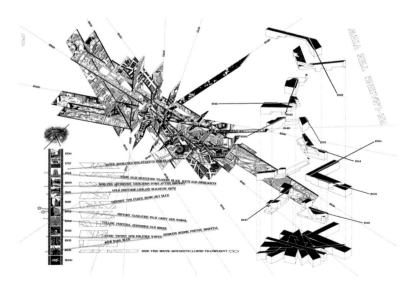

123457

Out of line
Potsdamer Platz, urban competition
Berlin, Germany, 1991
left conceptual drawing
right site plan with "Aleph Wing"

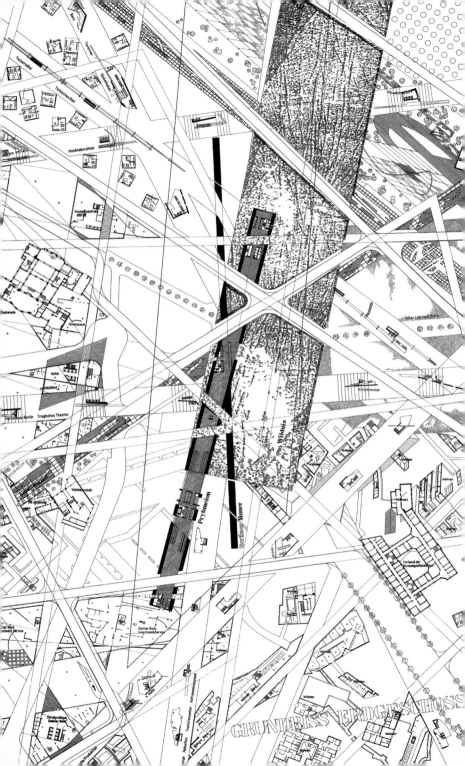

GRUNDRISS ERDGESCHOSS

Out of line
Potsdamer Platz, urban competition
Berlin, Germany, 1991
left Re-leasing the view.
Construction site as puzzle
right "Illuminated Muse Matrix"

123457

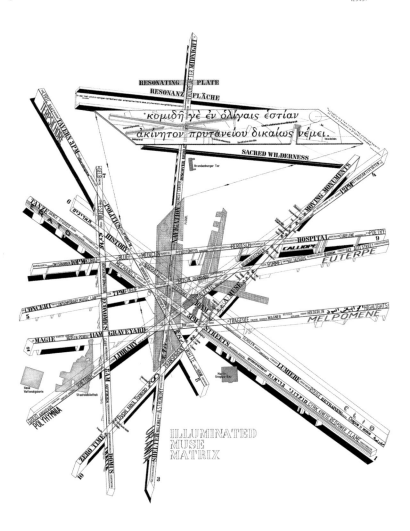

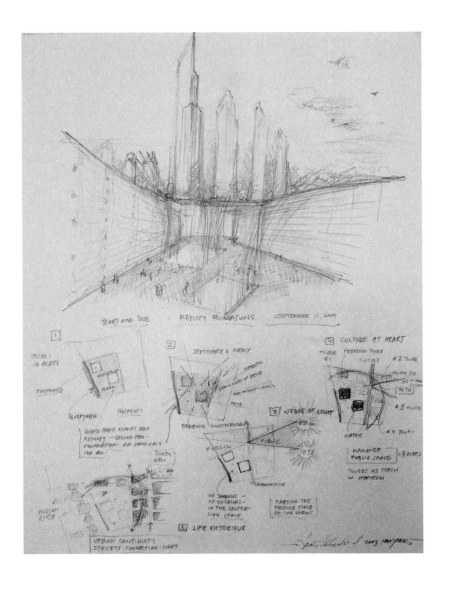

HEART AND SOUL : MEMORY FOUNDATIONS   SEPTEMBER 11, 2001

1   TOTAL:
16 ACRES

FOOTPRINTS

SLURRY WALL   FOOTPRINTS

VOID SPACE EXPOSES DEEP
MEMORY — GROUND ZERO
FOUNDATIONS OF DEMOCRACY
FOR ALL

2   SEPTEMBER 11 MATRIX

BEDROCK UNDERGROUND

PUBLIC   PUBLIC

3   WEDGE OF LIGHT
8:46 AM
10:28

NO SHADING —
NO BUILDINGS —
IN THE CENTER:
CIVIC SPACE

MARKING THE
PRECISE TIME
OF THE EVENT

4   CULTURE AT HEART
TOWER   FREEDOM TOWER
#1   CULTURE   #2 TOWER

PATH

#3 TOWER

WATER   #4 TOWER

MAXIMIZE
PUBLIC SPACE = 8 ACRES

TOWERS AS TORCH
IN HORIZON

HUDSON
RIVER

URBAN CONTINUITY
STREETS CONNECTION: LIGHT

5   LIFE VICTORIOUS

World Trade Center Master Plan
New York, USA, 2003
left Heart and soul: memory foundations
right site view

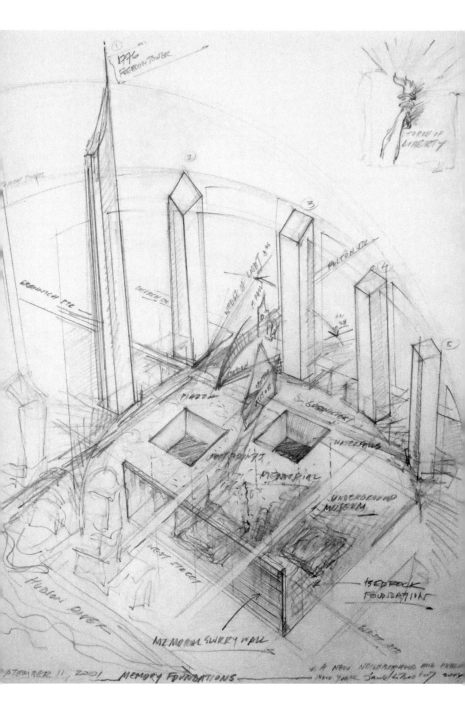

1796 FREEDOM TOWER

TORCH OF LIBERTY

GREENWICH STR.

WEDGE OF LIGHT 8AM

FULTON STR.

PIAZZA

S. GREENWICH

WATERFALLS

FOOTPRINTS

MEMORIAL

UNDERGROUND + MUSEUM

WEST STREET

BEDROCK FOUNDATIONS

HUDSON RIVER

MEMORIAL SLURRY WALL

SEPTEMBER 11, 2001   MEMORY FOUNDATIONS   A NEW NEIGHBORHOOD AND PUBLIC
NEW YORK   DANIEL LIBESKIND 2004

NEW YORK
MEMORY FOUNDA

World Trade Center Master Plan
New York, USA, 2003
previous pages a new neighborhood and public space
these pages site sketch, place center, spiral movement

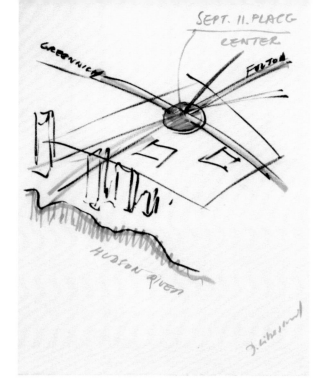

SEPT. 11. PLACG
CENTER

GREENWICH

FULTON

HUDSON RIVER

D. Libeskind

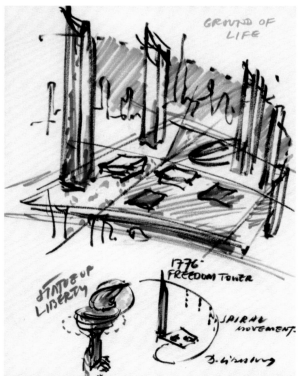

GROUND OF LIFE

STATUE OF LIBERTY

1776 FREEDOM TOWER

SPIRAL MOVEMENT.

D. Libeskind

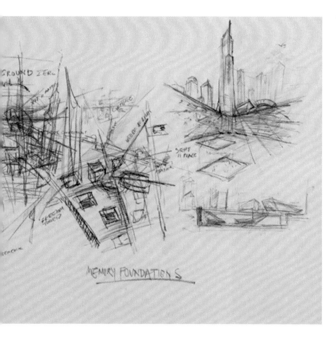

**World Trade Center
Master Plan**
New York, USA, 2003
study sketches

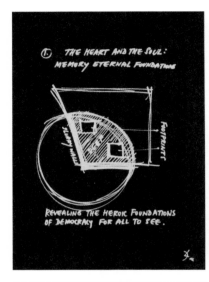

① THE HEART AND THE SOUL:
MEMORY ETERNAL FOUNDATIONS

REVEALING THE HEROIC FOUNDATIONS
OF DEMOCRACY FOR ALL TO SEE.

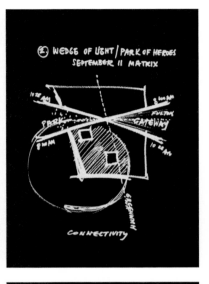

② WEDGE OF LIGHT / PARK OF HEROES
SEPTEMBER 11 MATRIX

CONNECTIVITY

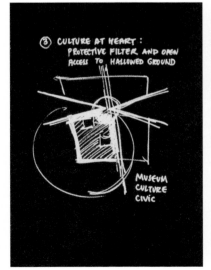

③ CULTURE AT HEART:
PROTECTIVE FILTER AND OPEN
ACCESS TO HALLOWED GROUND

MUSEUM
CULTURE
CIVIC

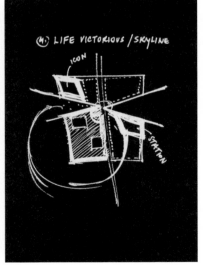

④ LIFE VICTORIOUS / SKYLINE

World Trade Center Master Plan
New York, USA, 2003
left design matrixes
right sketch

SUNLIGHT ON SEPTEMBER 11
MARKING THE <u>PRECISE</u>
TIME OF THE EVENT.

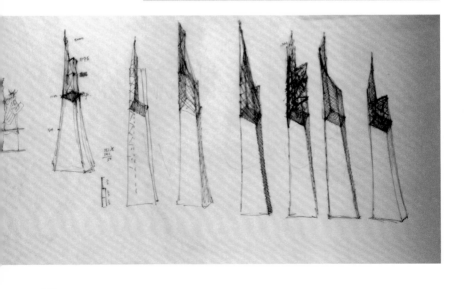

World Trade Center Master Plan
New York, USA, 2003
Freedom Tower and Statue of Liberty studies

THE SOUL OF SEOUL

THE MOUNTAINS

THE SOUL

THE PARK

THE HAN

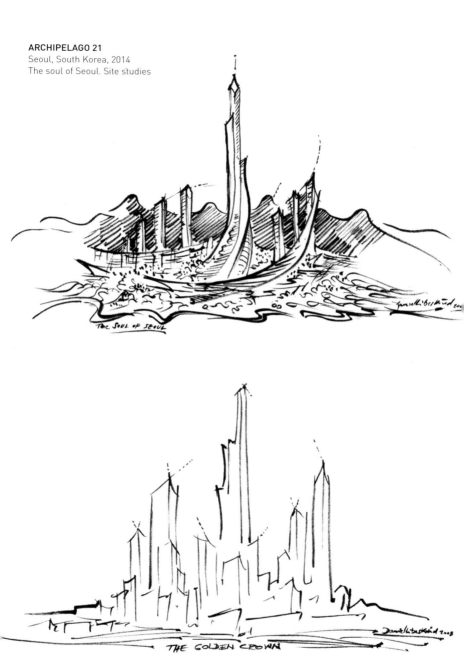

ARCHIPELAGO 21
Seoul, South Korea, 2014
The soul of Seoul. Site studies

THE SOUL OF SEOUL

THE GOLDEN CROWN

ARCHIPELAGO 21
Seoul, South Korea, 2014
left concept drawings
right design matrixes

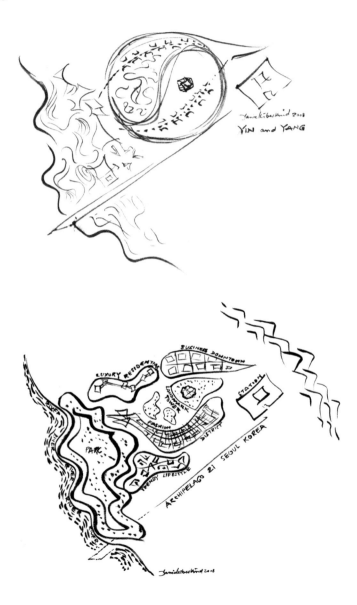

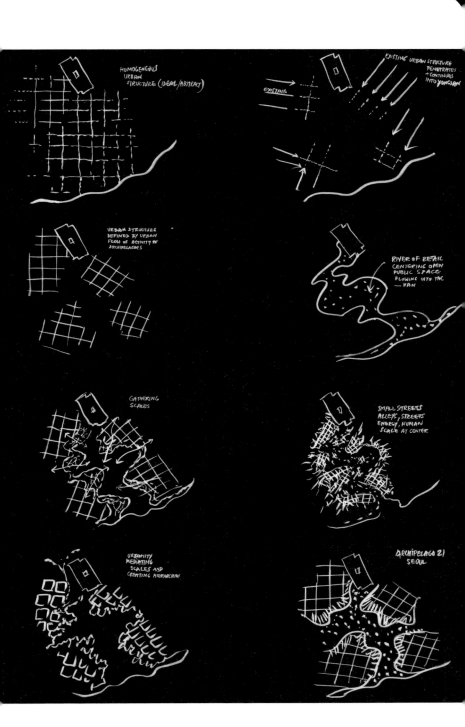

HOMOGENEOUS URBAN STRUCTURE (IDEAL/ABSTRACT)

EXISTING

EXISTING URBAN STRUCTURE PENETRATES + CONTINUES INTO YONGSAN

URBAN STRUCTURE DEFINED BY URBAN FLOW OF ACTIVITY OF ARCHIPELAGOES

RIVER OF RETAIL CENTERING OPEN PUBLIC SPACE FLOWING INTO THE — HAN

GATHERING SCALES

SMALL STREETS ALLEYS, STREETS ENERGY, HUMAN SCALE AT CENTER

URBANITY MEDIATING SCALES AND CREATING HIERARCHY

ARCHIPELAGO 21 SEOUL

105

Architectural Explorations 3
Chamber Works

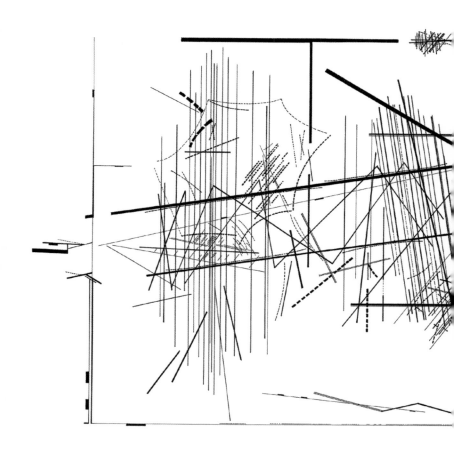

Chamber Works
Horizontal series
Drawings, 1983

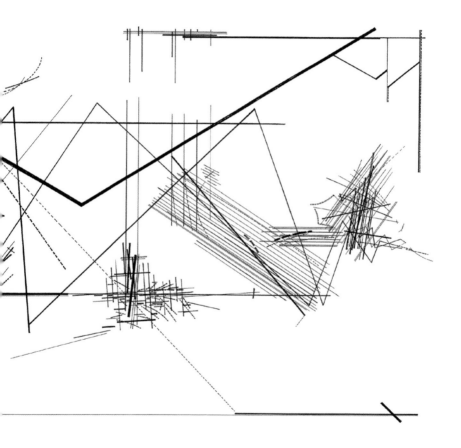

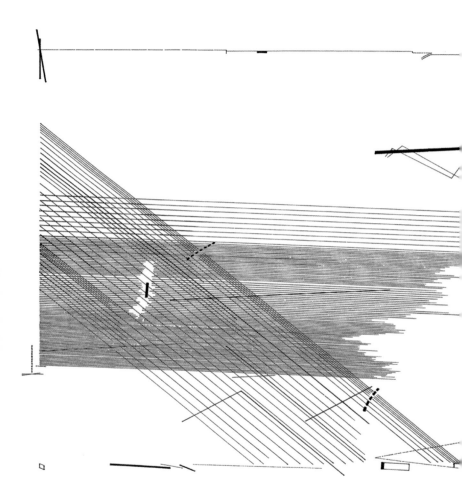

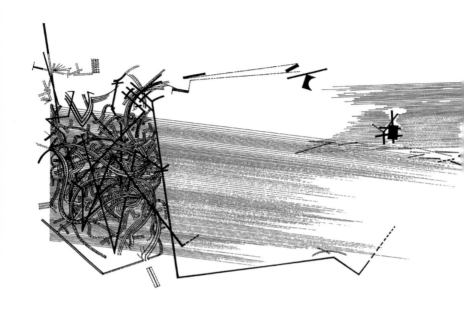

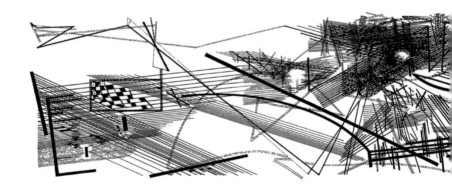

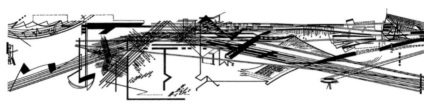

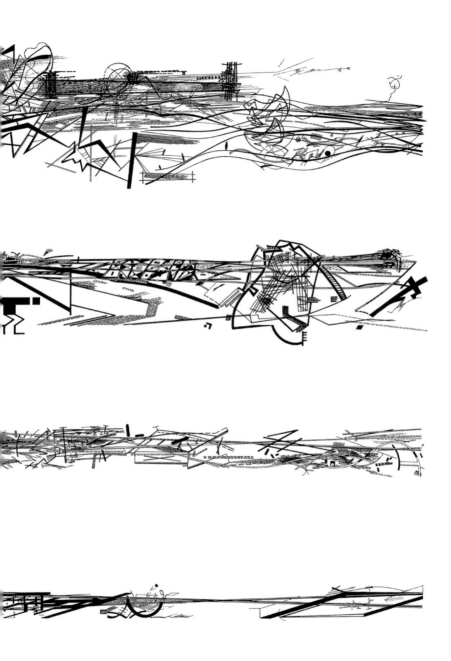

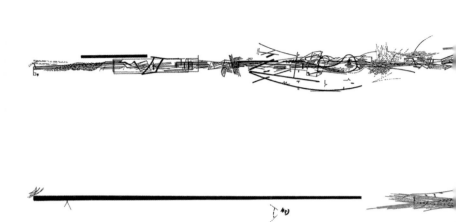

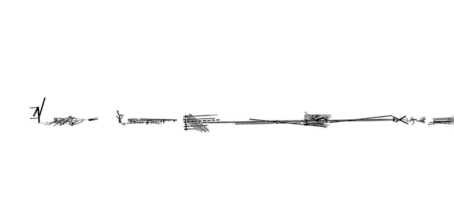

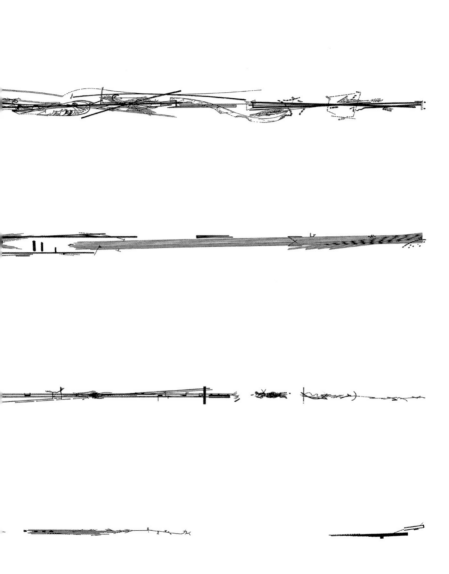

Design Process 3
Towers

The more recent of Libeskind's works seem to be sustained by and driven towards an organic three-dimensionality projected skywards. In these drawings one senses a fascination for a certain proportion, in spite of the unpredictable distortion in volumes. One is witness to leaps and falls that will characterize the final result in a not unequivocal manner, making it hard to discern a path of assembly that was so meticulously probed and expressed in his previous works. The typical mark of the architect, employed with an unprecedented and subversive complexity in the theoretical inquiries and in the initial project developments, gives way to a simplification of the lines and signs that succeeds in evoking icons more than the project in its multifaceted intricacy.

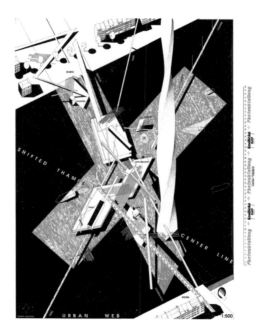

**Thames Habitable
Bridge competition**
London, UK, 1996
left urban web
right vertical bridge

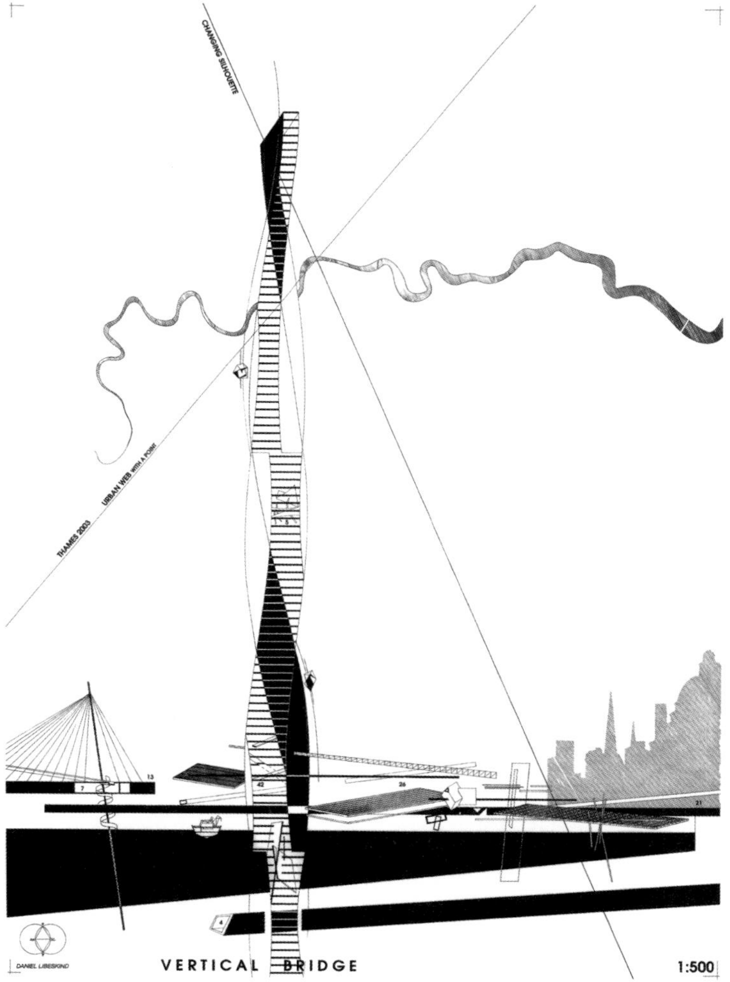

CHANGING SILHOUETTE

THAMES 2003   URBAN WEB WITH FLOW

VERTICAL BRIDGE

DANIEL LIBESKIND

1:500

New York Tower
New York, USA, 2008
study sketches

PARK HYATT SEOUL®

995-14 Daechi 3-dong, Gangnam-gu, Seoul, 135-502, Korea
TELEPHONE +82 2 2016 1234 FACSIMILE +82 2 2016 1200
ROOM RESERVATIONS +82 2 2016 1100
seoul.park.hyatt.com

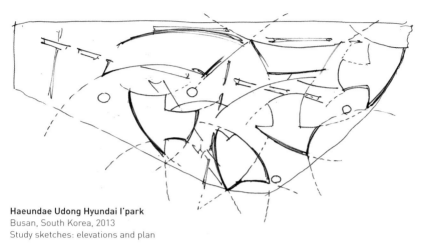

Haeundae Udong Hyundai I'park
Busan, South Korea, 2013
Study sketches: elevations and plan

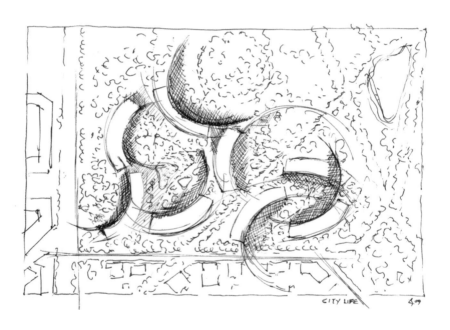

CITY LIFE

Citylife
Milan, Italy, 2005-2017
masterplan, Residences
and Central Tower C

MILANO

Zlota
Warsaw, Poland, 2015
study sketches

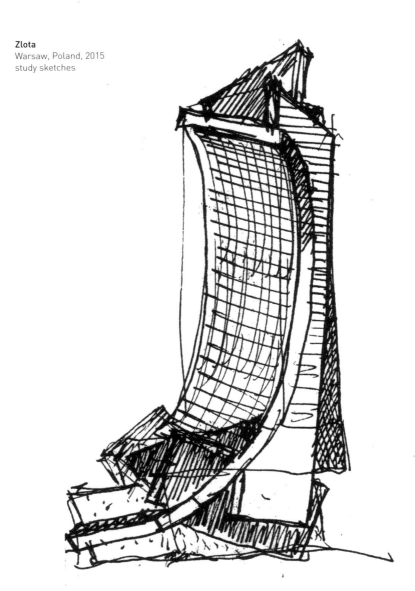

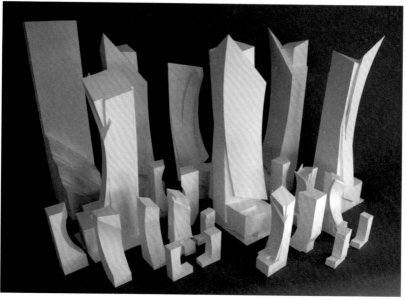

Zlota
Warsaw, Poland, 2015
urban view

Architectural Explorations 4
Sonnets in Babylon

Sonnets in Babylon marks Libeskind's return to the search for an architecture investigated through drawing of a non-figurative kind. This is a series of 100 drawings executed by hand with a pen, watercolours and coffee grounds, exhibited in 2014 at the Venice Biennial and screen-printed onto glass plates of large dimensions. They are inspired by a verse from a Shakespearean sonnet as well as by the complex architecture of the Tower of Babel. The point, line and surface used in the architectural explorations of the 1980s give way to biomorphic fragments, frameworks, connections and abstractions. The sequence of drawings constitutes the scenes of a drama in which we recognize the contradictory complexity of the contemporary.

Sonnets in Babylon
Drawings, 2011
right Wind, often enough,
causes a rotten standstill

following pages
Slow red is our "ought"

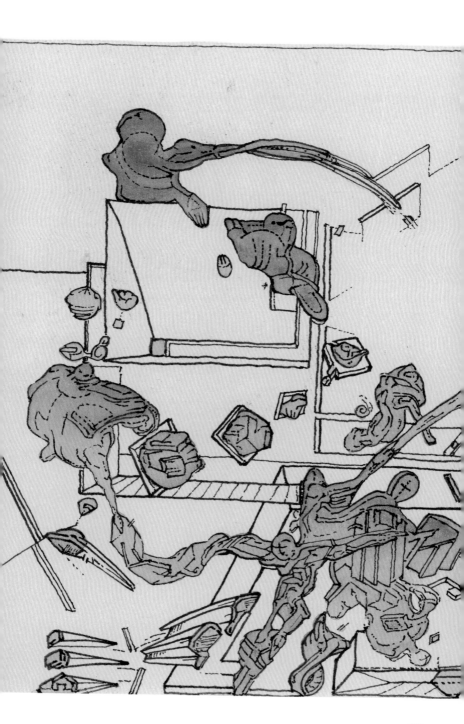

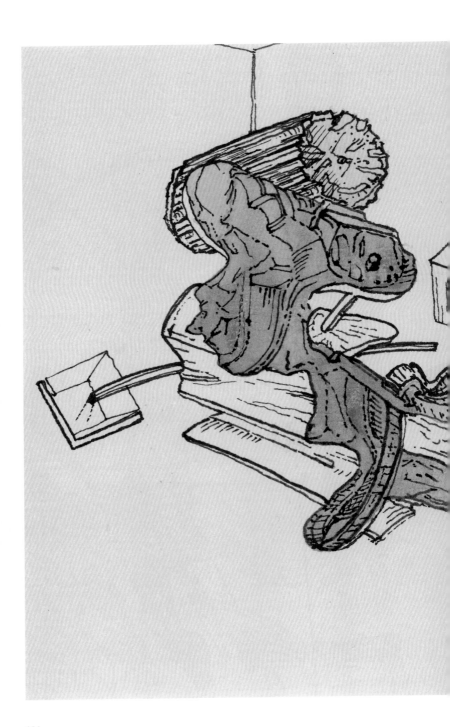

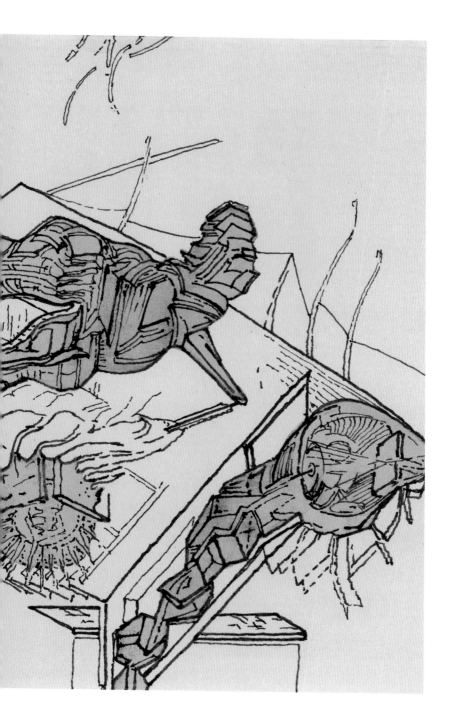

Sonnets in Babylon
Drawings, 2011
left The world naively desires
right Stay vigilant if honored

following pages
Erect shapes in the sinciput

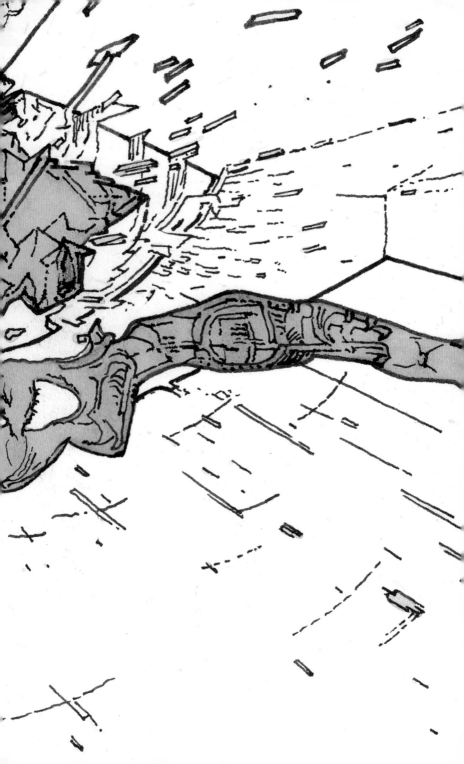

Sonnets in Babylon
Drawings, 2011
Many sit like the figure 8 (parallel a's)

Biography

An international figure in architecture and urban design, the architect Daniel Libeskind is renowned for his ability to evoke cultural memory in buildings of equilibrium-defying contemporaneity. Informed by a deep commitment to music, philosophy, and literature, Mr. Libeskind aims to create architecture that is resonant, original, and sustainable. Born in Lód'z, Poland, in 1946, Mr. Libeskind immigrated to the United States as a teenager. He received the American-Israel Cultural Foundation Scholarship and performed as a musical virtuoso, before eventually leaving music to study architecture. He received his professional degree in architecture from the Cooper Union for the Advancement of Science and Art in 1970 and a postgraduate degree in the history and theory of architecture from the School of Comparative Studies at Essex University in England in 1972.

Daniel Libeskind established his architectural studio in Berlin, Germany, in 1989 after winning the competition to build the Jewish Museum. In February 2003, the Studio moved its headquarters from Berlin to New York City when Daniel Libeskind was selected as the master planner for the World Trade Center redevelopment. The practice is involved in designing and realizing a diverse array of urban, cultural and commercial projects internationally and it has completed buildings that range from museums and concert halls to convention centers, university buildings, hotels, shopping centers and residential towers.

As Principal Design Architect for Studio Libeskind, Mr. Libeskind speaks widely on the art of architecture in universities and professional summits. His architecture and ideas have been the subject of many articles and exhibitions, influencing the field of architecture and the development of cities and culture. Mr. Libeskind lives in New York with his wife and business partner, Nina Libeskind.

Credits

Francesca Serrazanetti
PhD in Architecture, she lectures and
researches at the Department of Architecture
and Urban Studies at the Politecnico di Milano.
She works as independent curator on
exhibitions and publishing projects,
writing on architecture, design and theatre.
She is editor of the magazine 'Stratagemmi'.

Matteo Schubert
Director of the culture department of ABCittà
s.c.r.l. and the architecture firm Alterstudio
Partners srl, with which he has carried
out numerous cultural and architectural
projects for private and public sector clients,
winning national and international awards.
He has developed and curated various events,
exhibitions and publications.

Other authors:

Danielle Rago
Danielle Rago is an independent architecture
and design curator based in Los Angeles.
She has worked with A+D Architecture and
Design Museum and LACMA in Los Angeles
and the Metropolitan Museum of Art and the
Guggenheim Museum in New York. She is
also a freelance contributor to a number of
international publications on art, architecture,
and design. Her writing has been published in
Abitare, Architect Magazine, Domus, Log, PIN-
UP, and Wired, among others.